made weight

RR
RHEINTAL Bank

MAGIC F

GERSTAFFEL
ESSERN
SwissLife
W&W
WINF

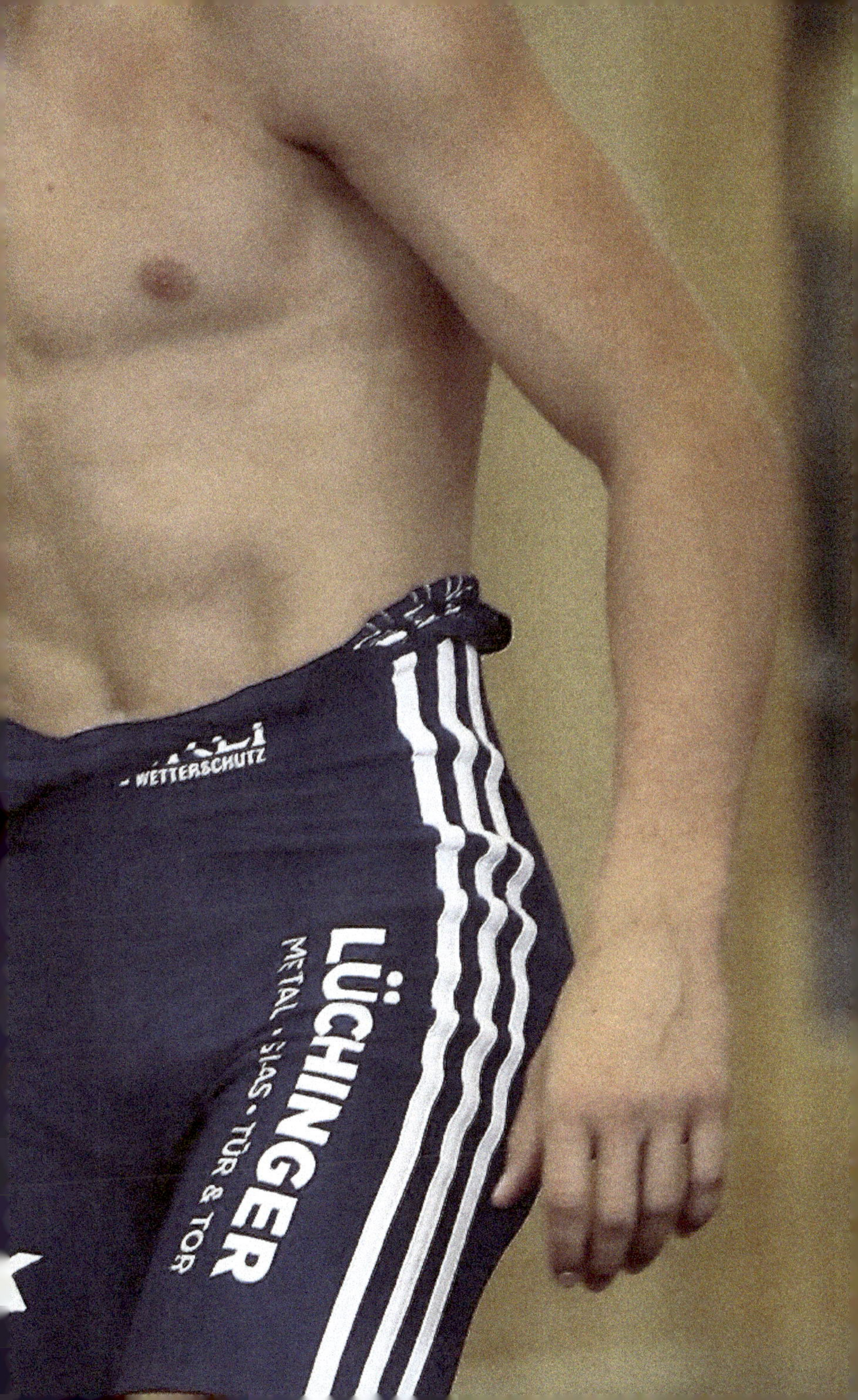
WETTERSCHUTZ
LÜCHINGER
TÜR & TOR

snack bar
FOX-FIGHT

Rössli

adidas

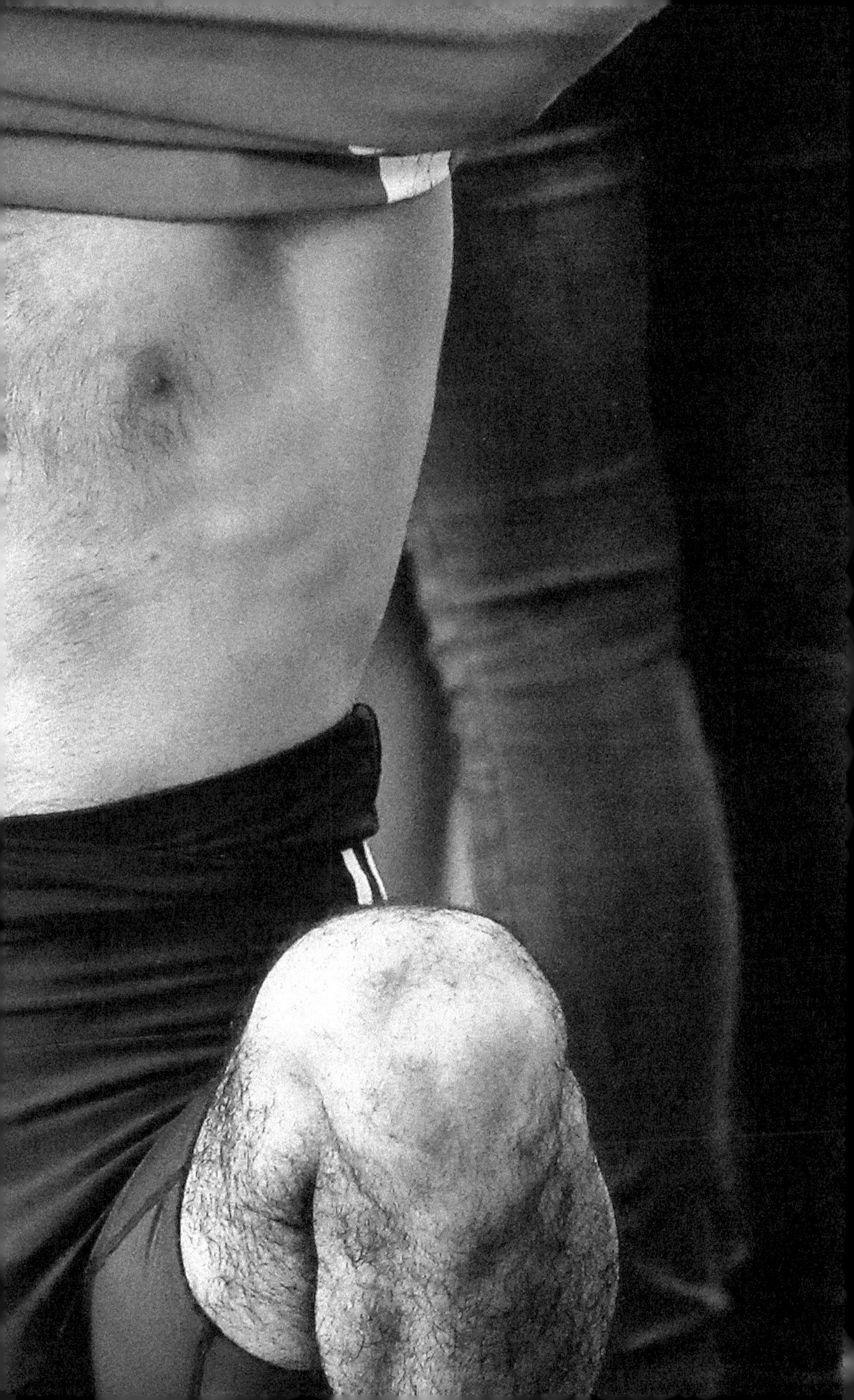

V R

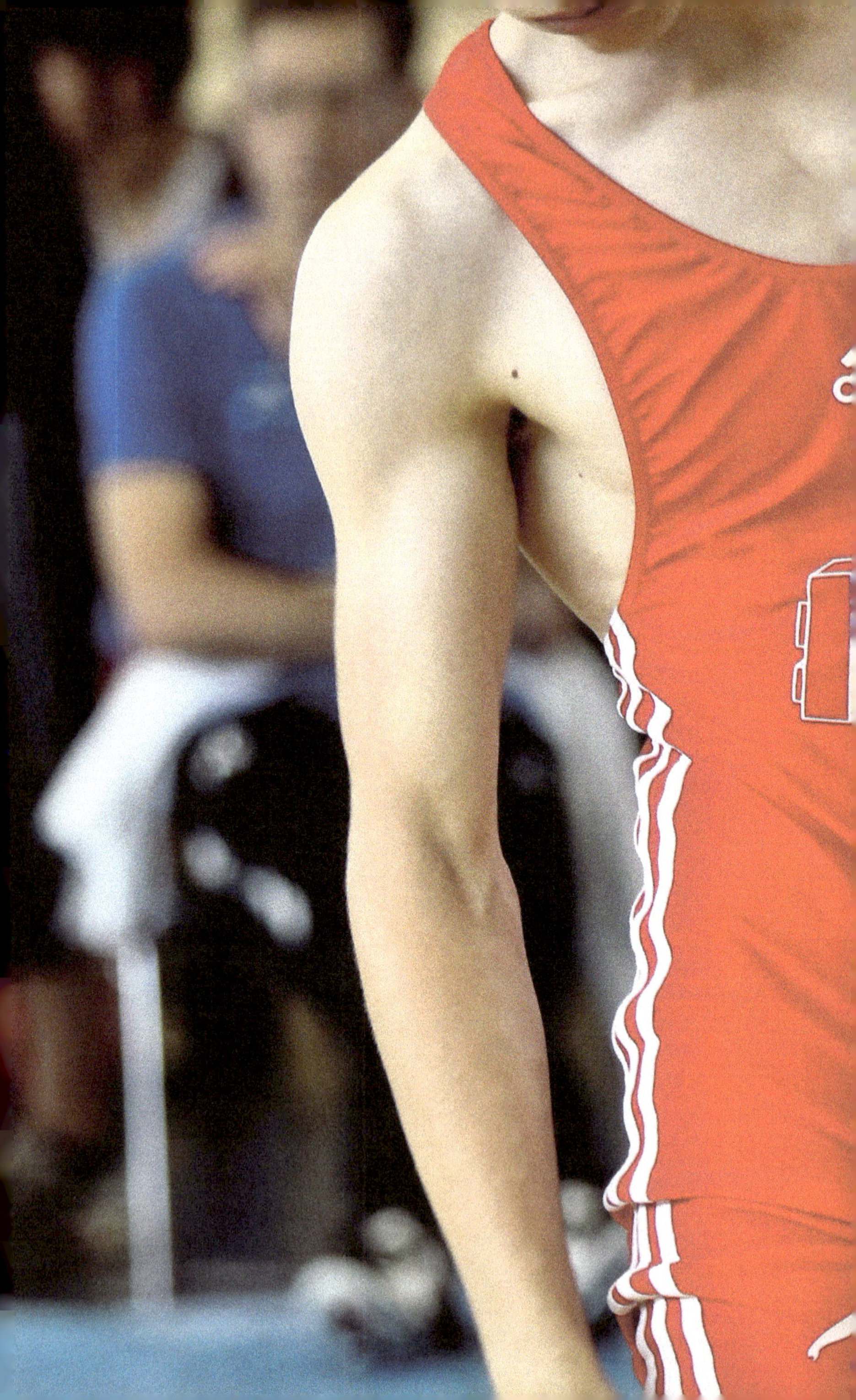

Raumausstattung
Achberger
Hörbranz

MAGIC FIT

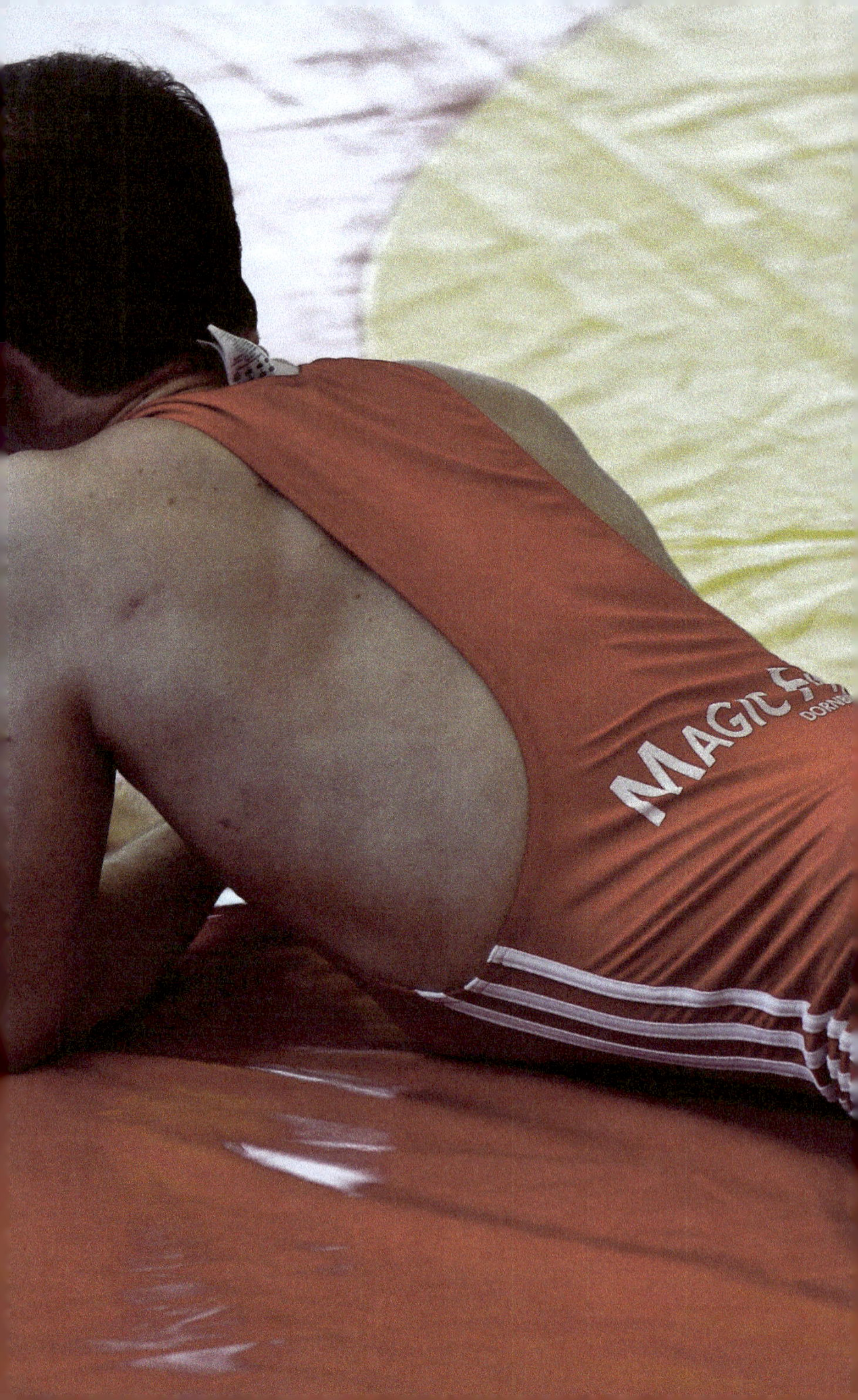
MAGIC

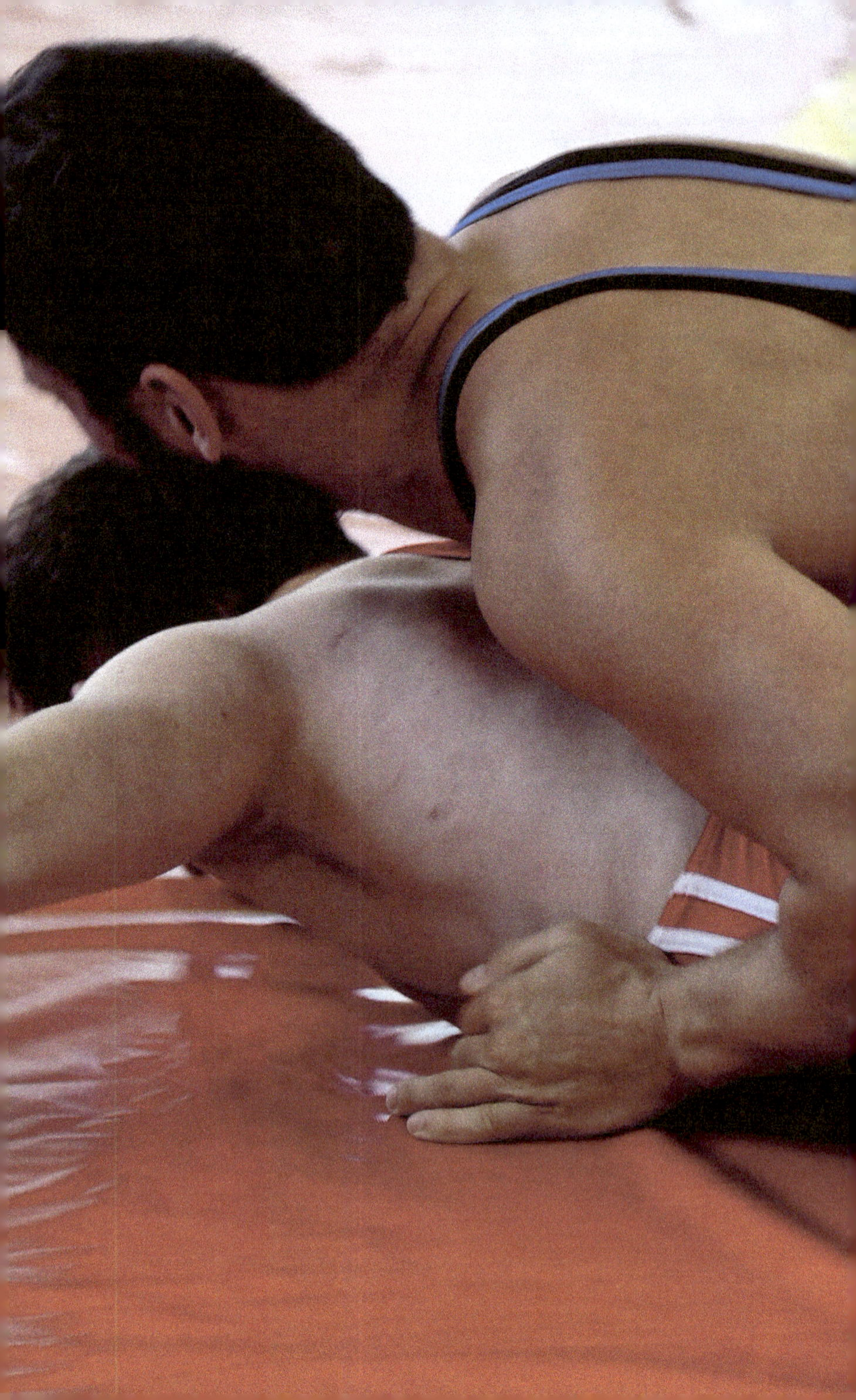

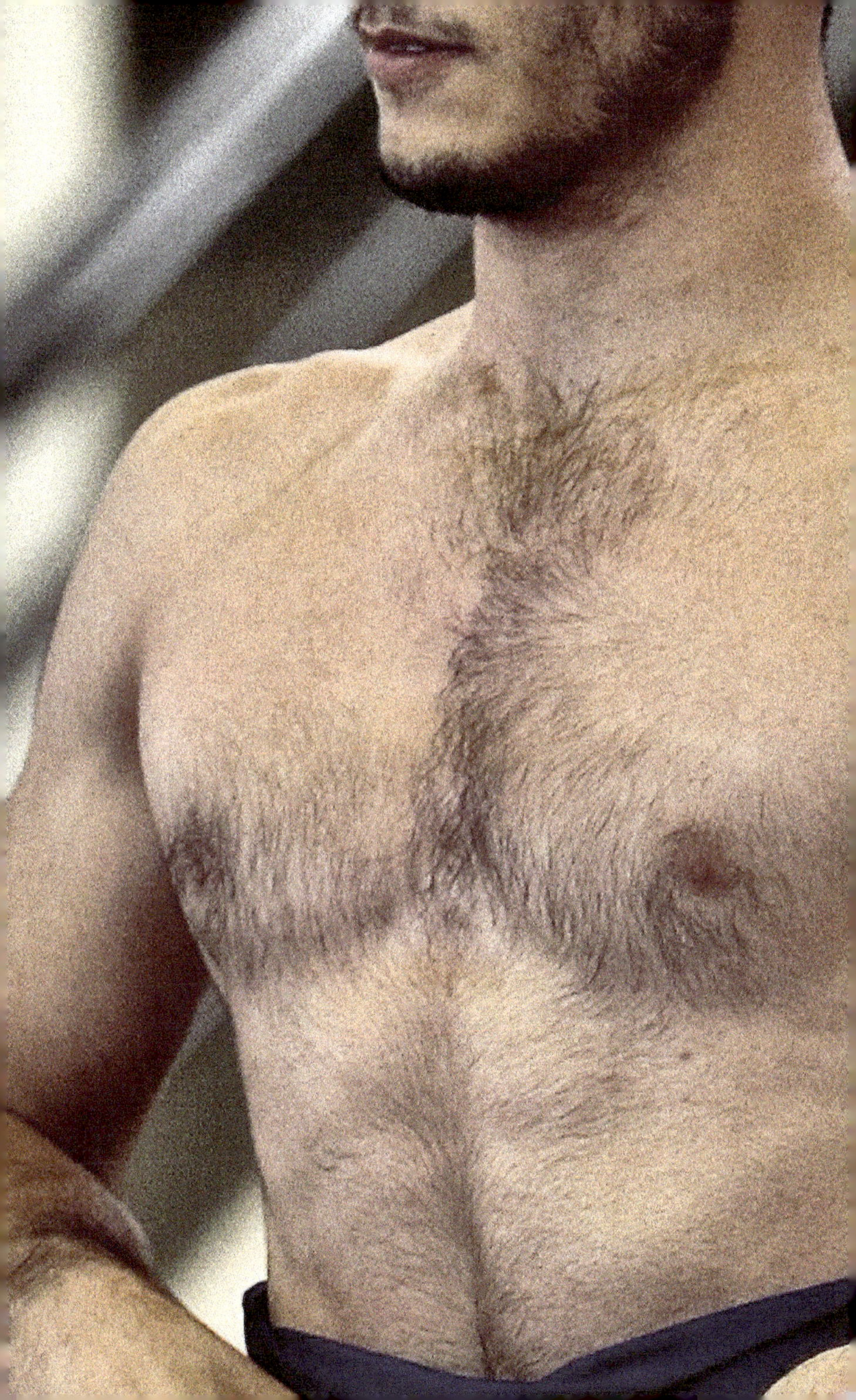

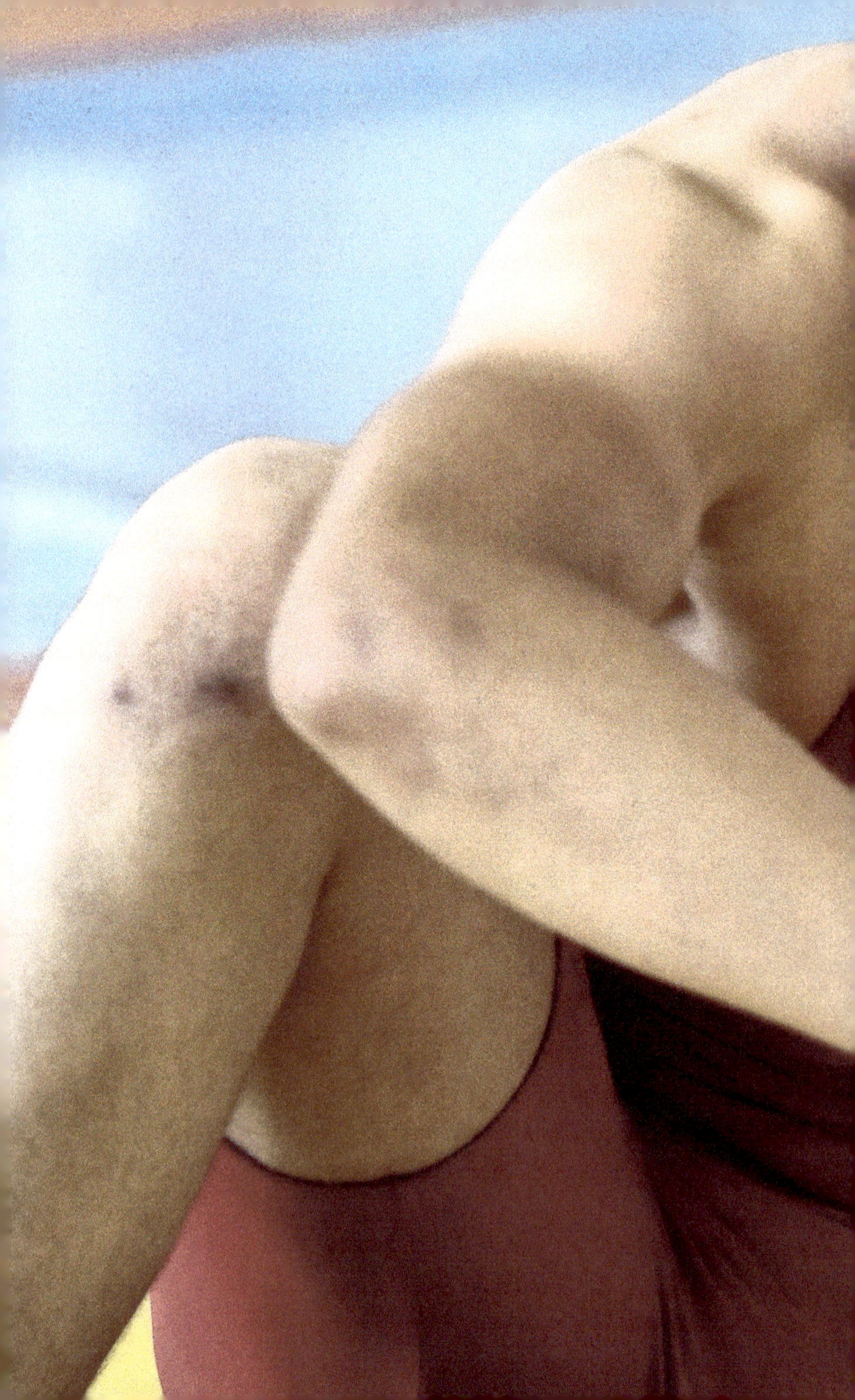

asics

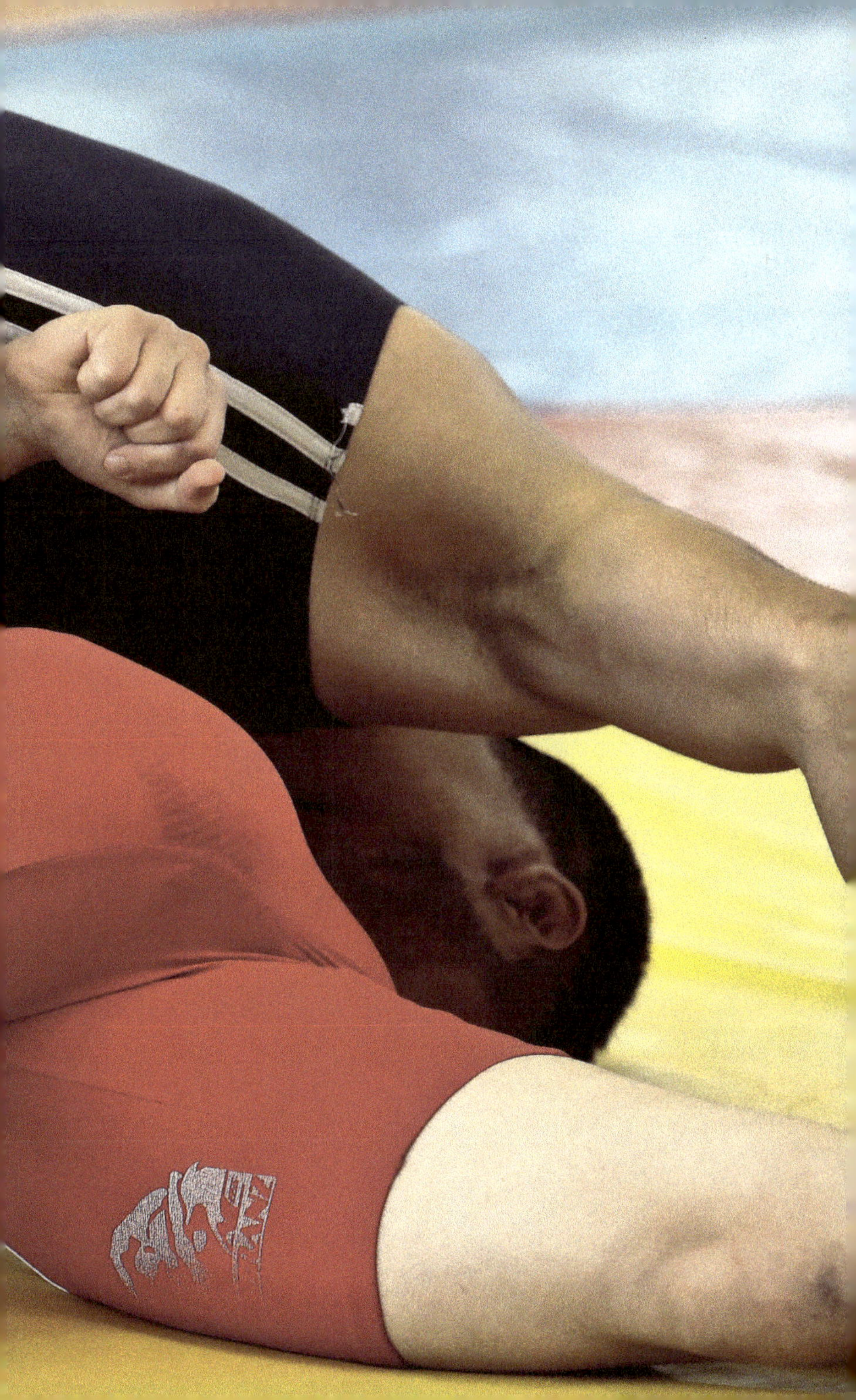

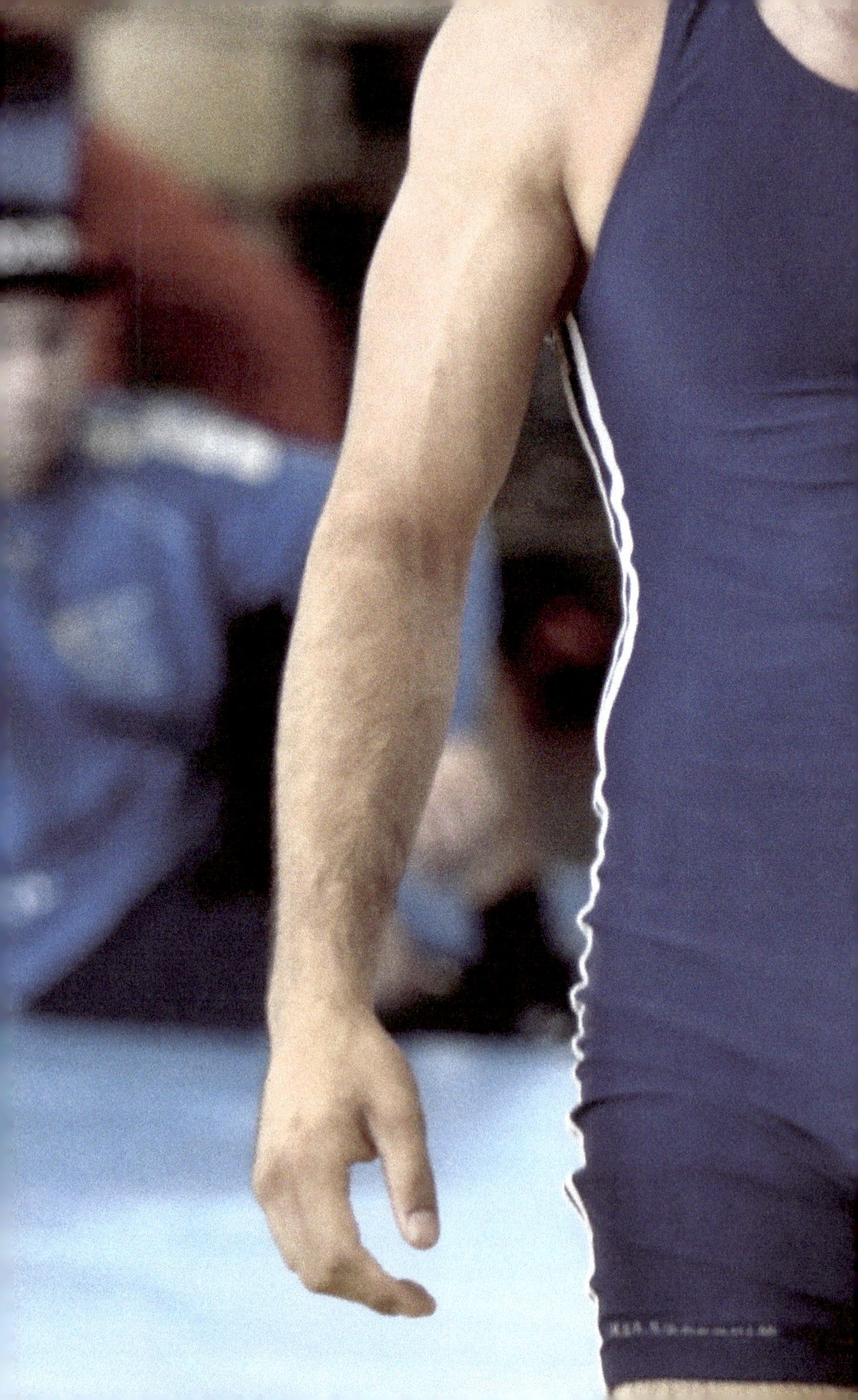

MATFLEX

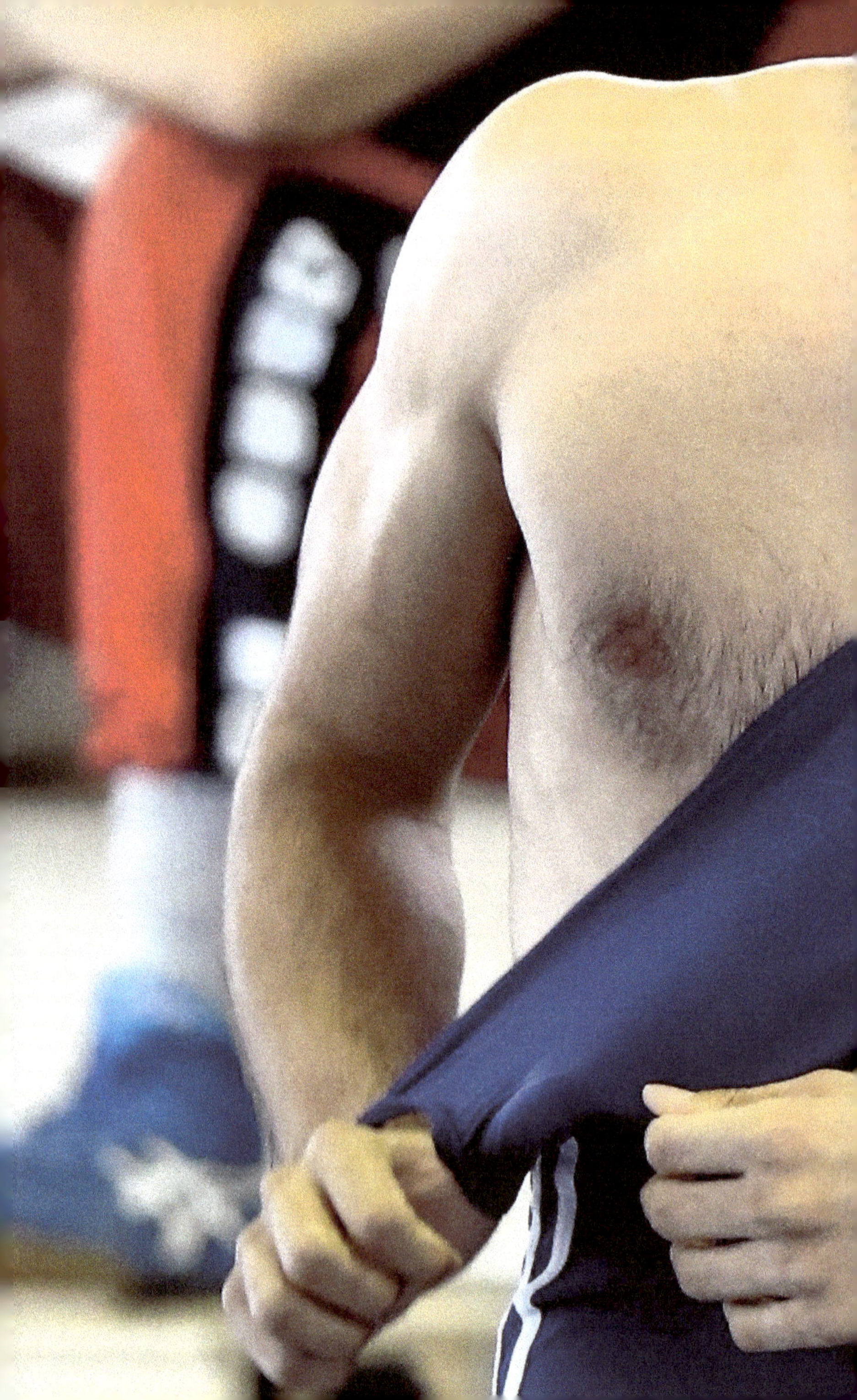

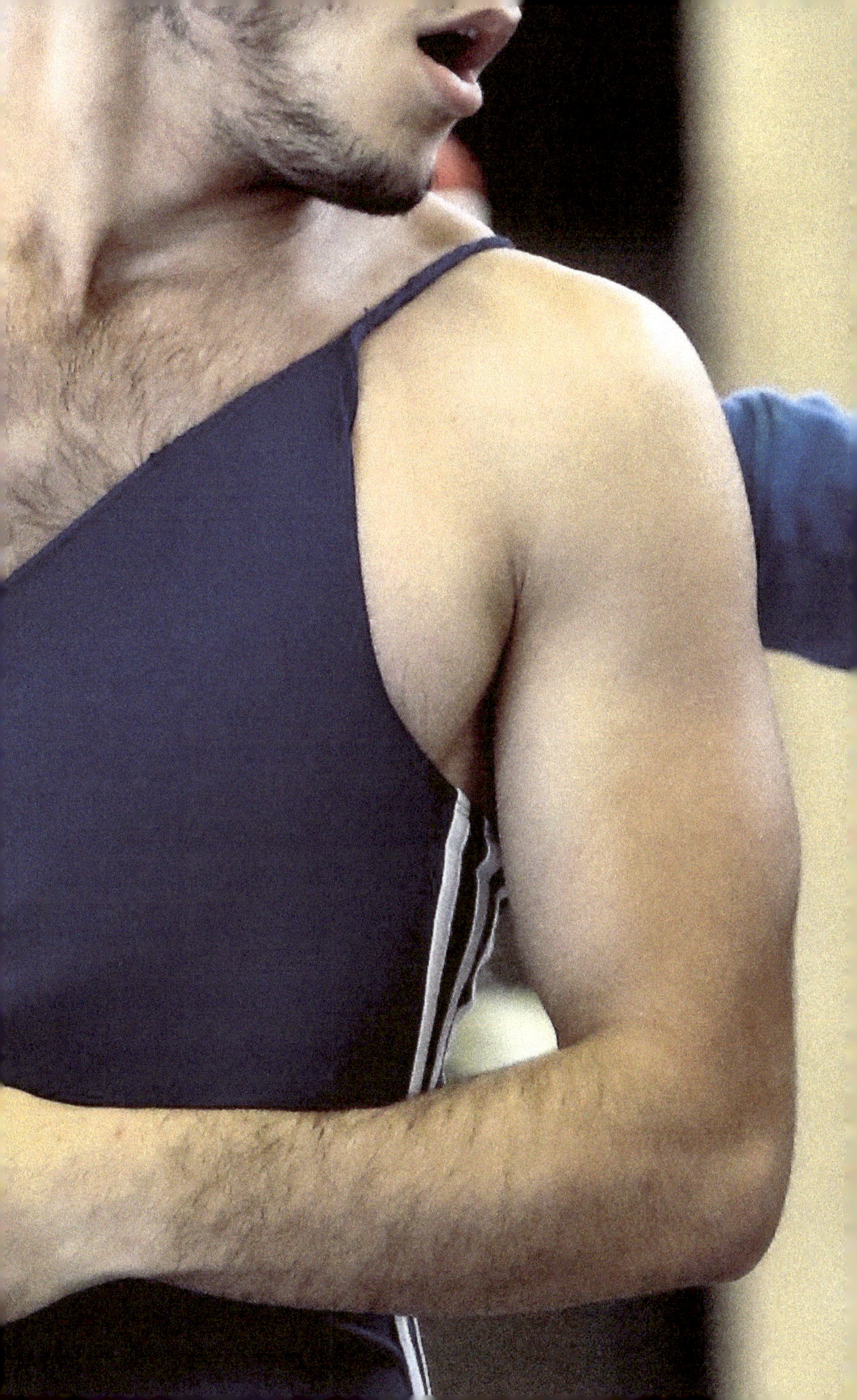

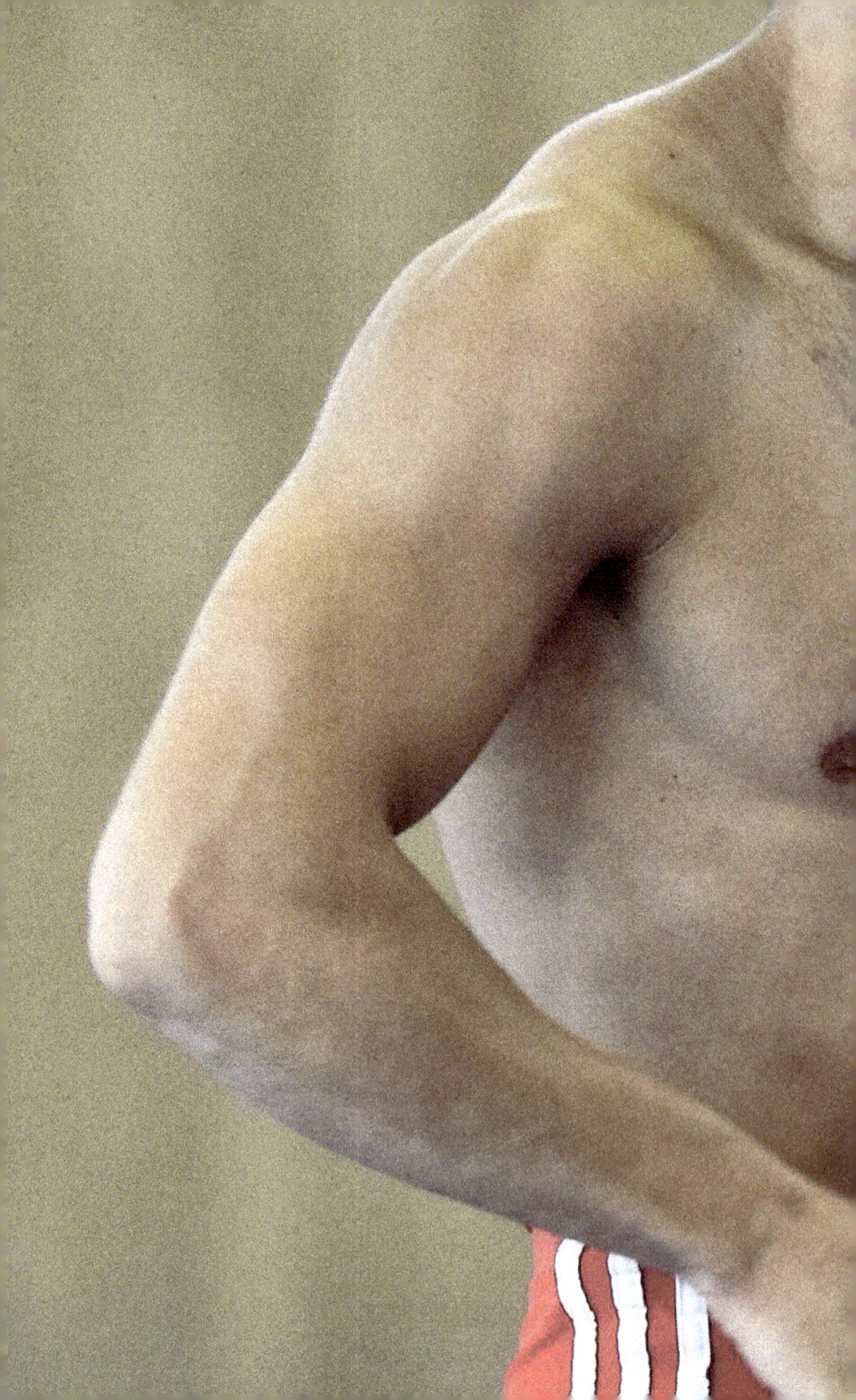

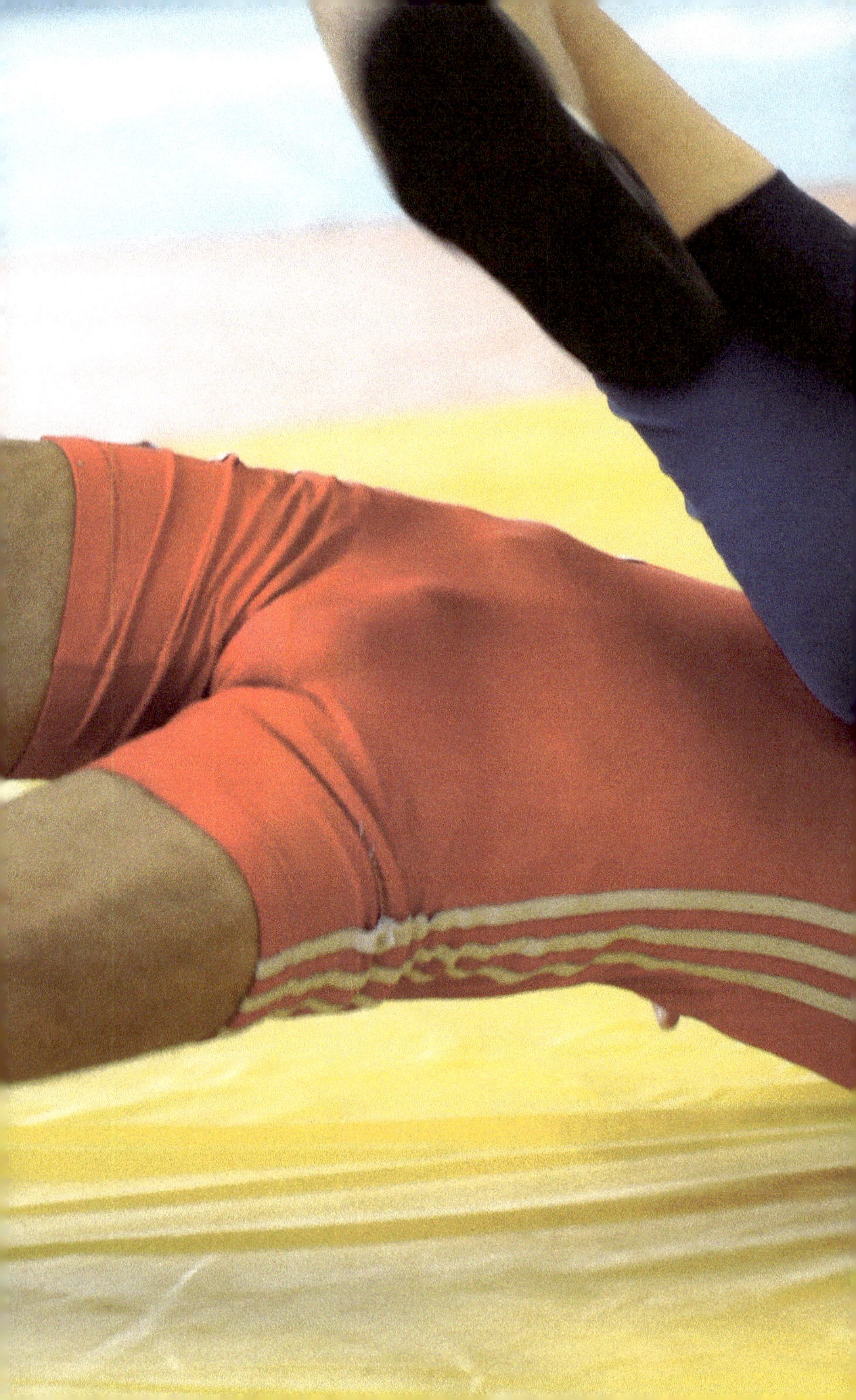

adidas

adidas

adidas

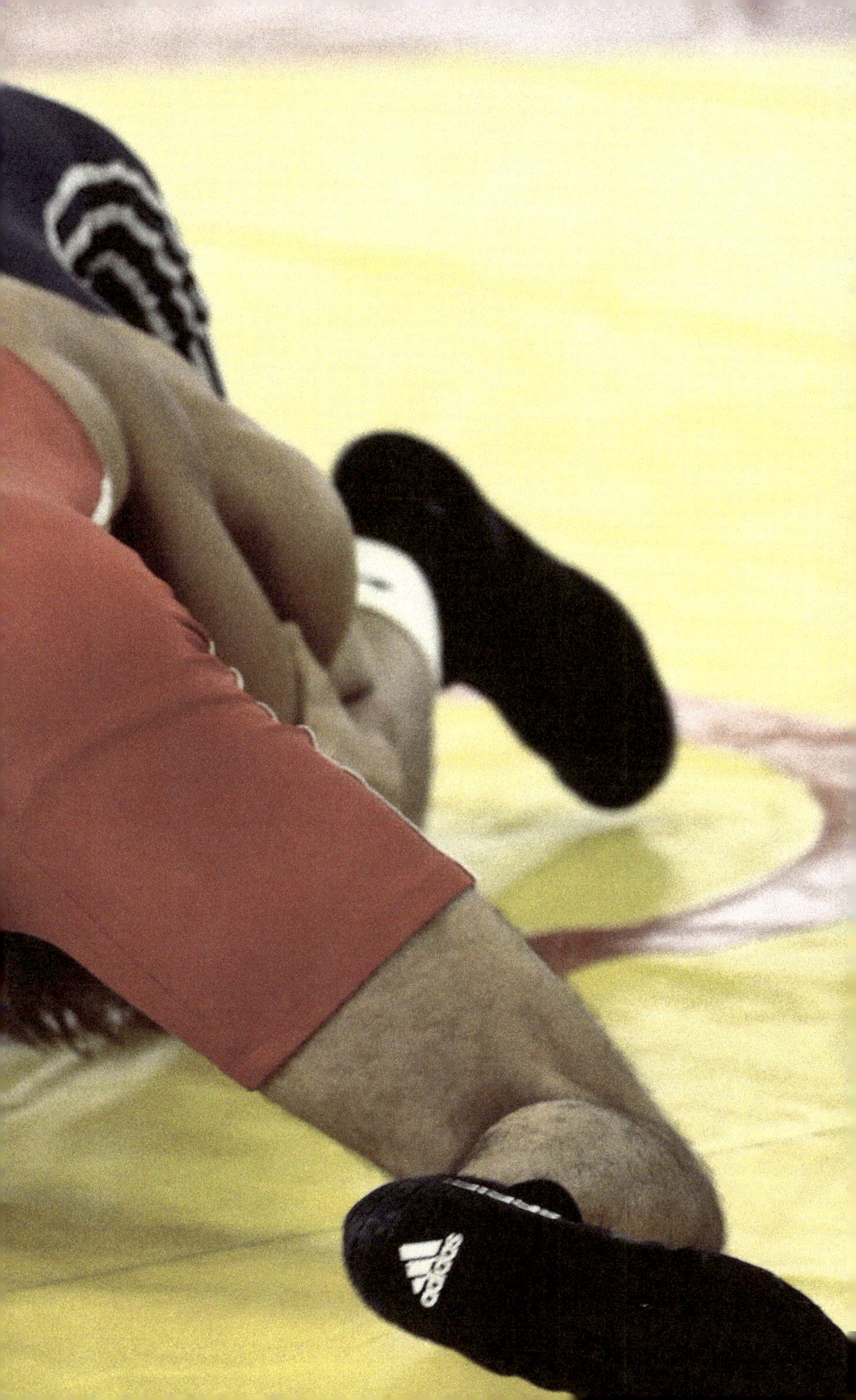
adidas

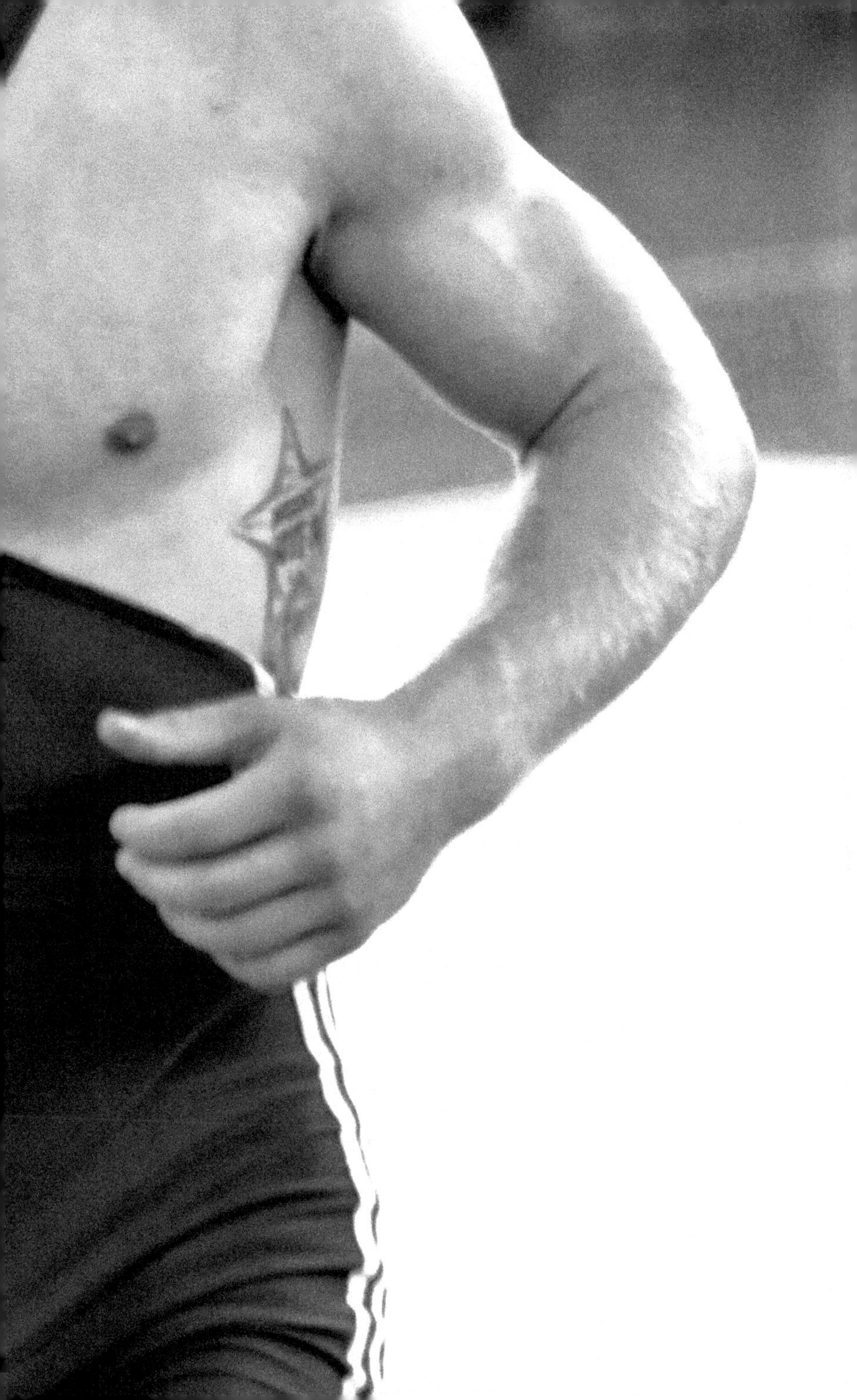

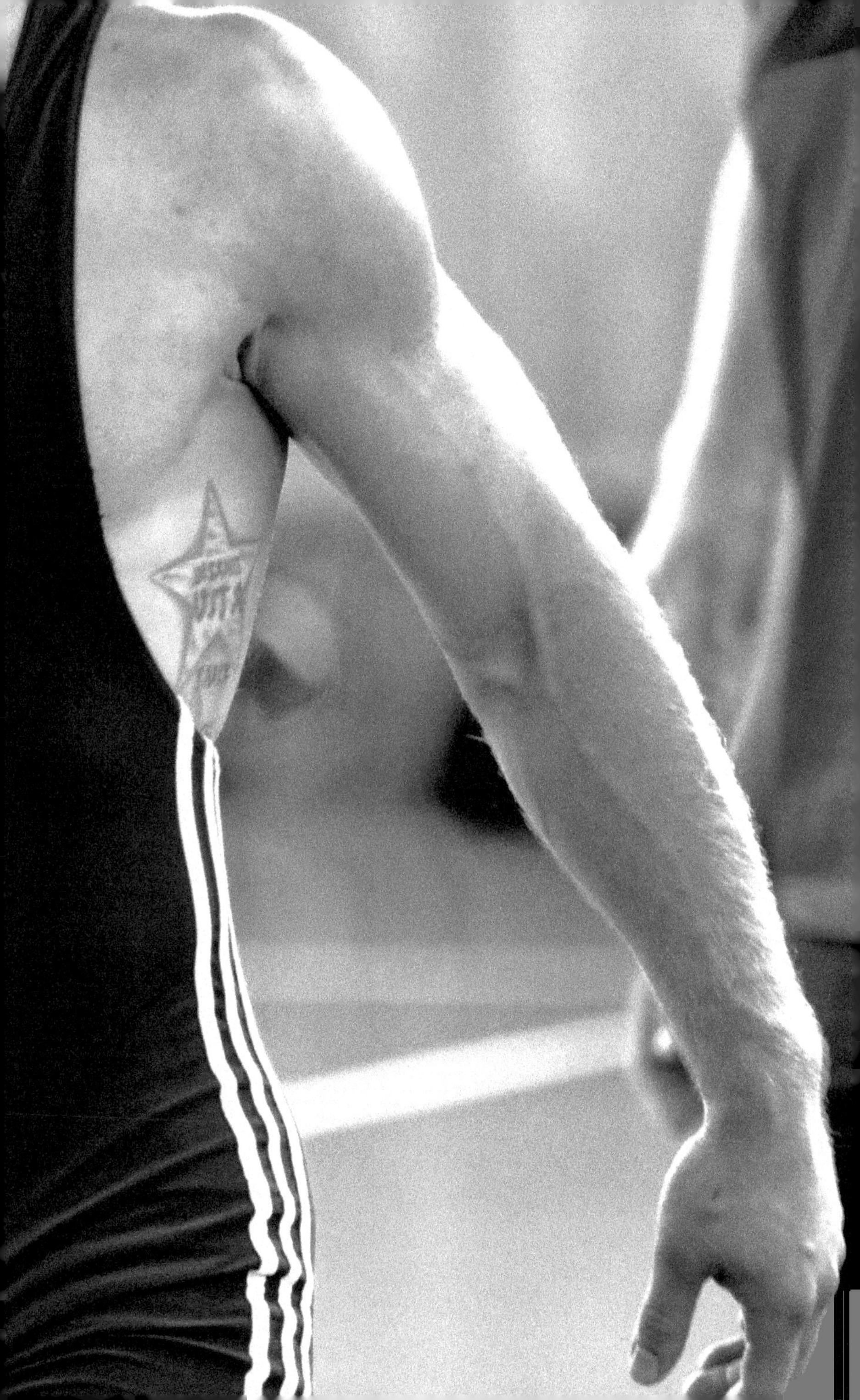

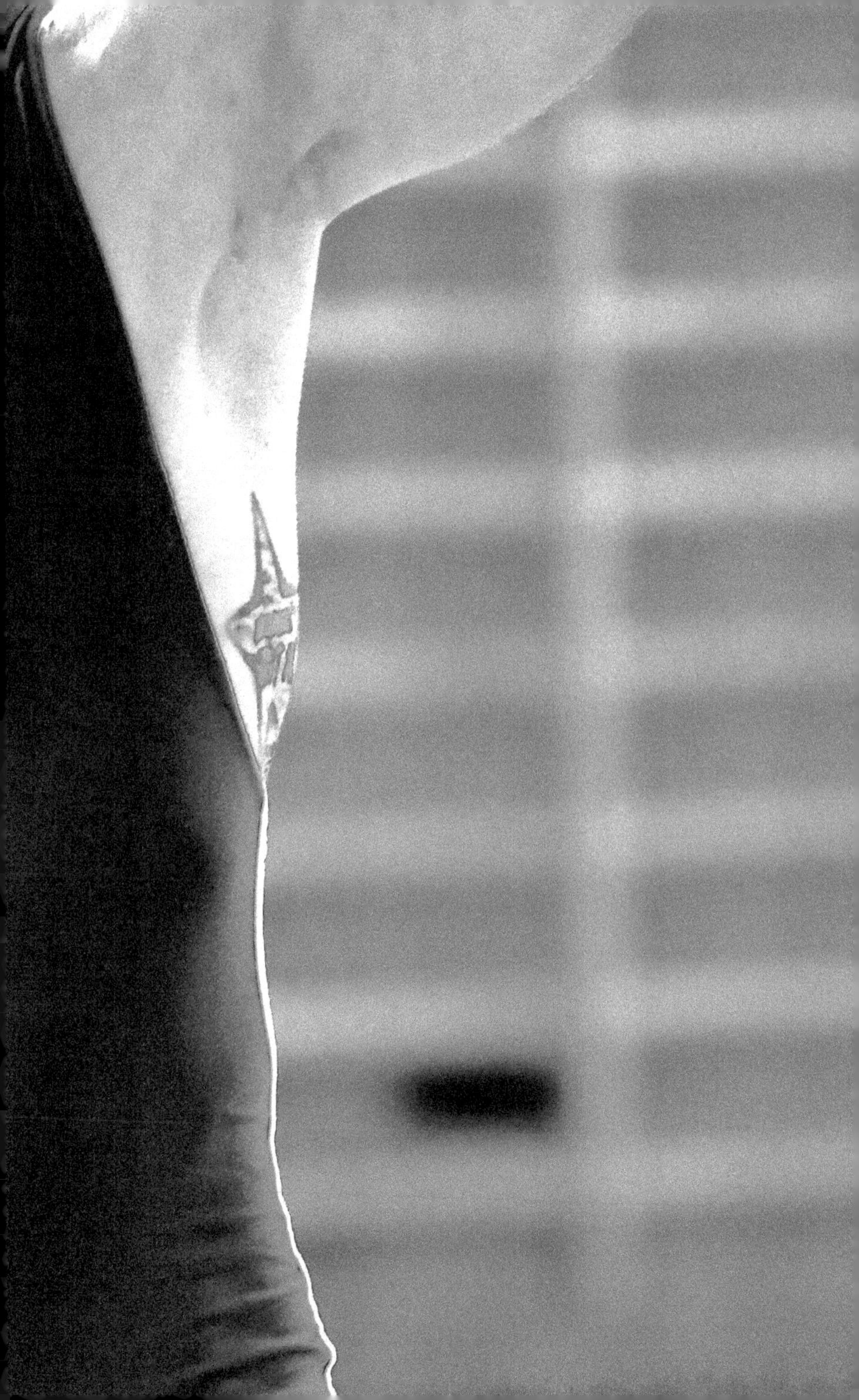

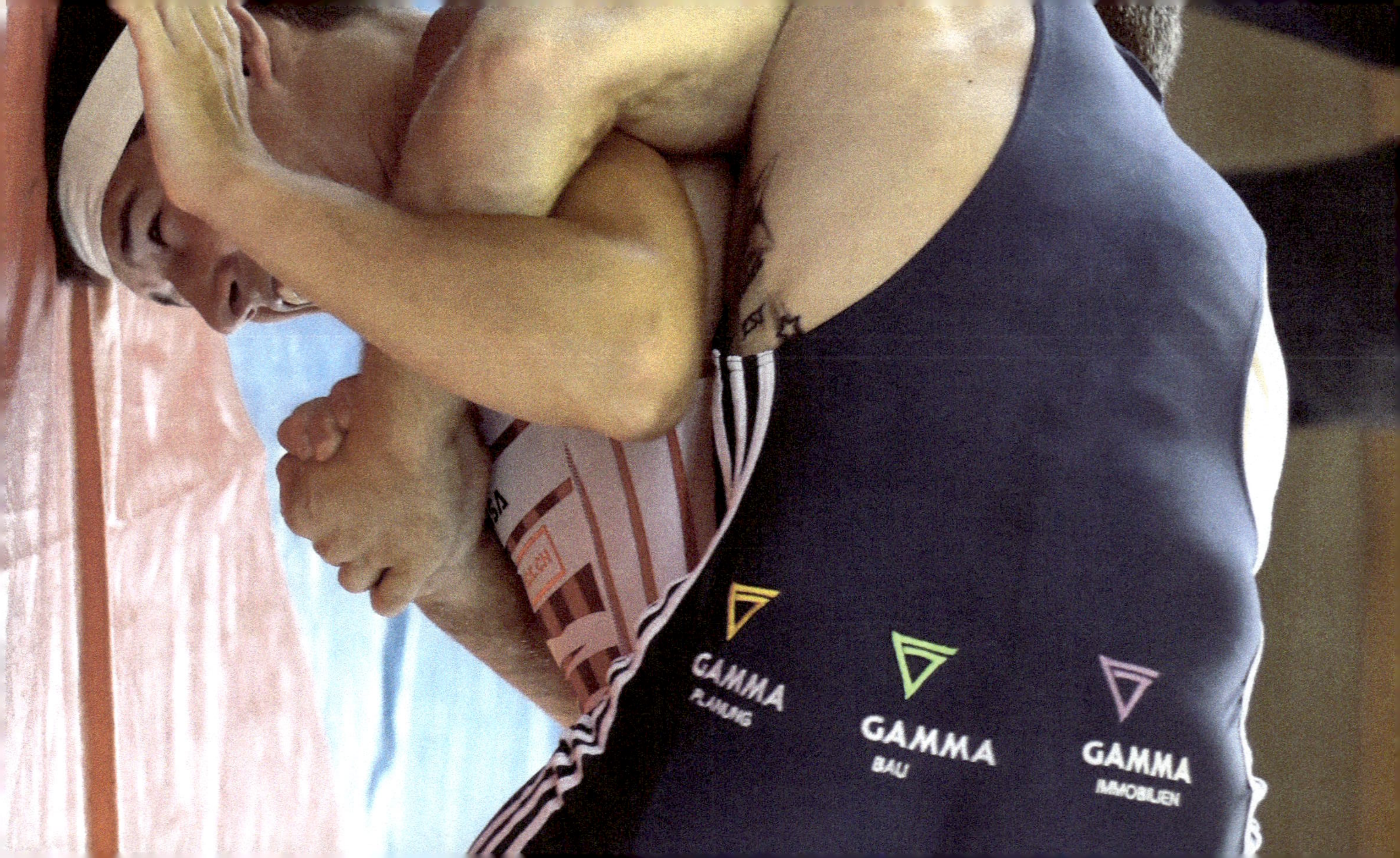
GAMMA
PLANUNG
GAMMA
BAU
GAMMA
IMMOBILIEN

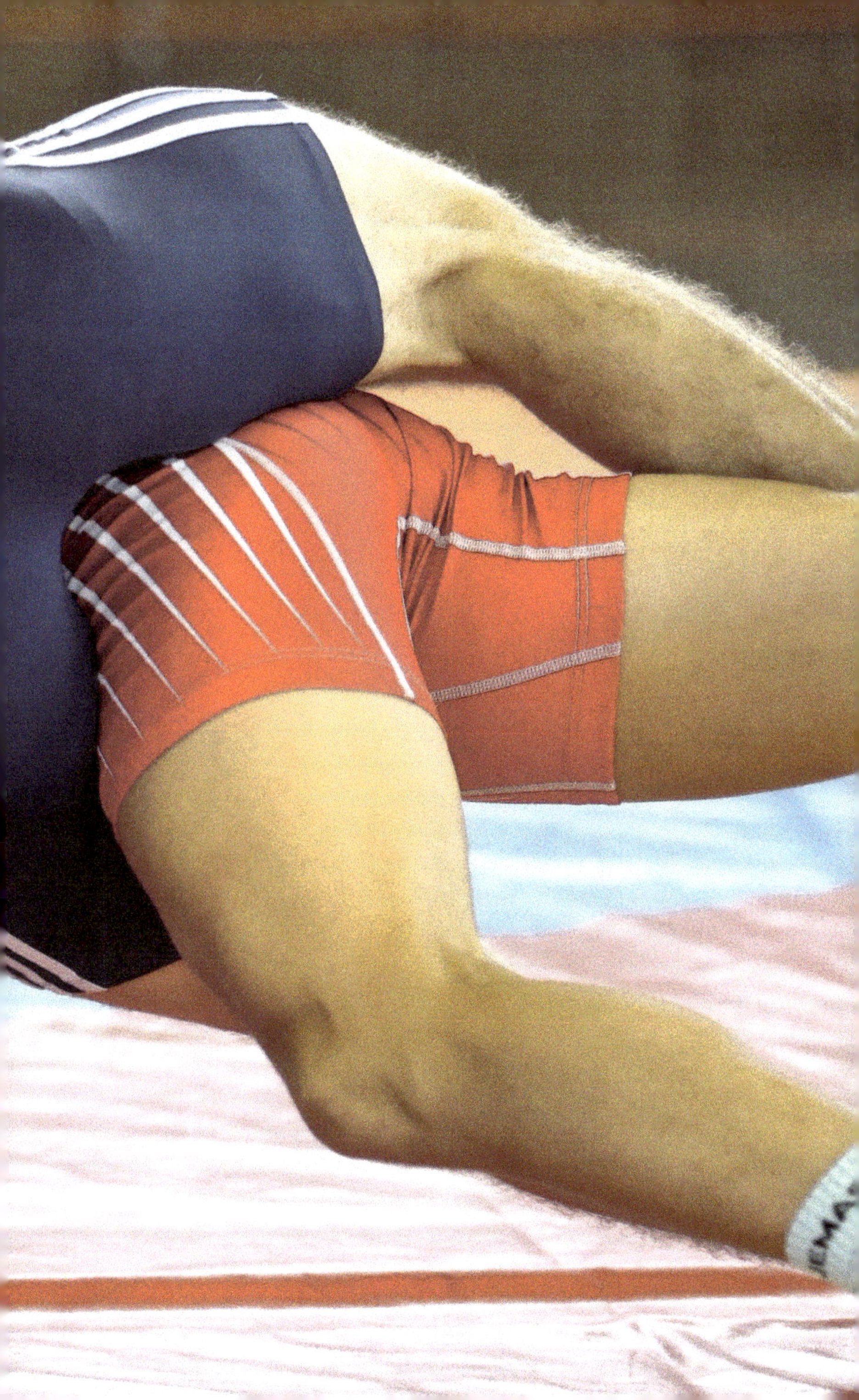

GAMMA
GAMMA
BAU

GAMMA
GAMMA
BAU

LIONS

GAMMA

GAM
BAU

GAMMA
IMMOBILIEN

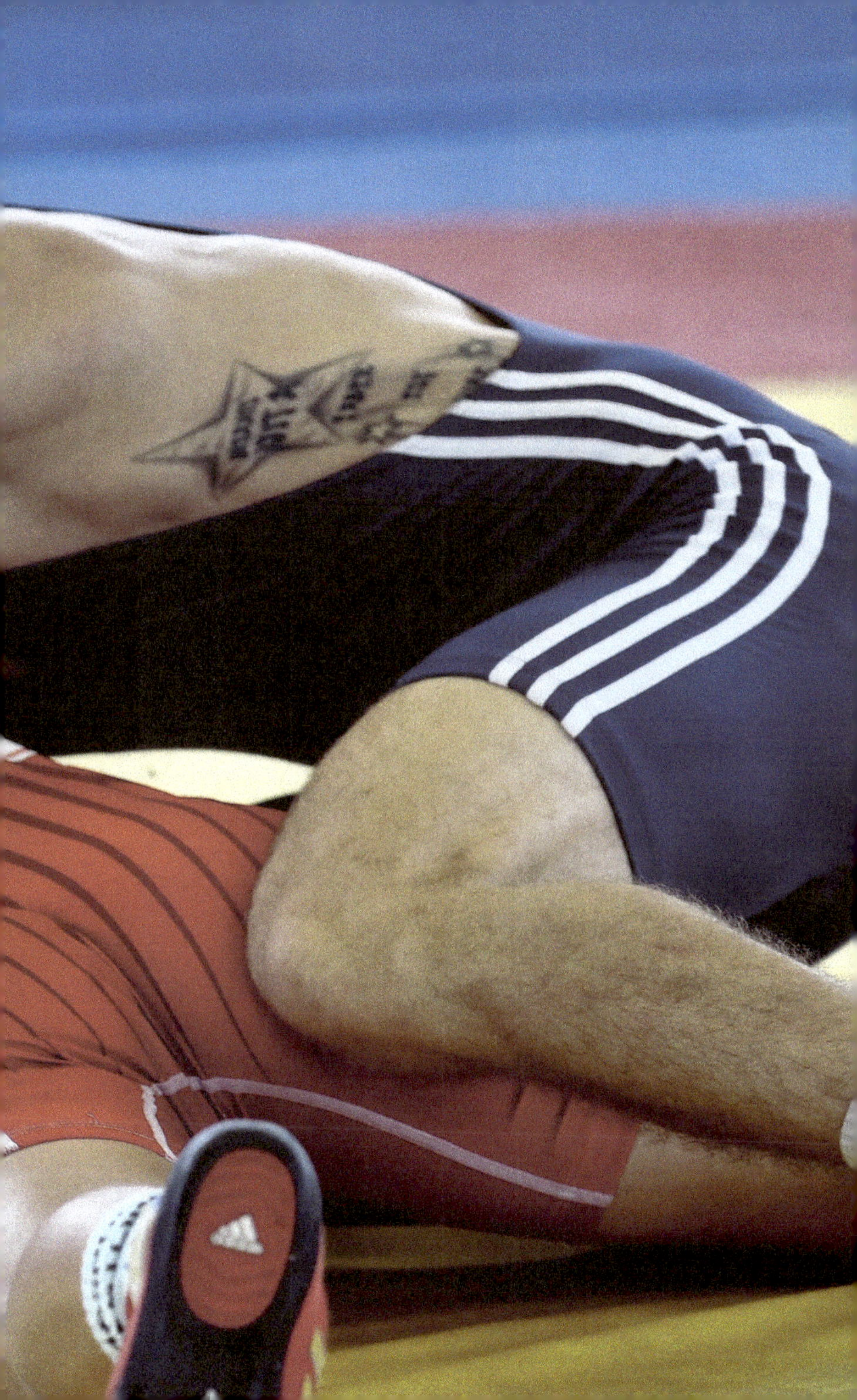

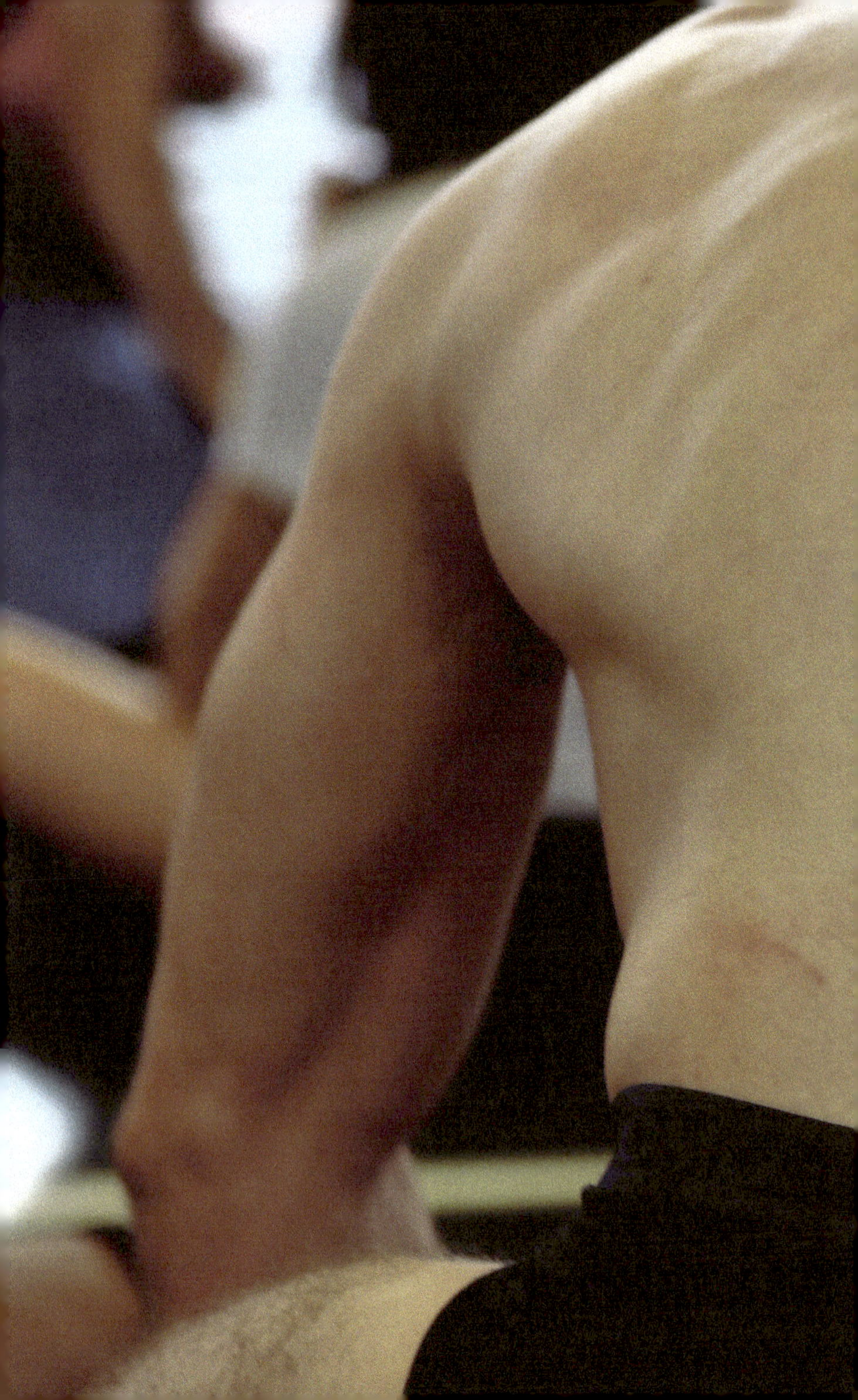

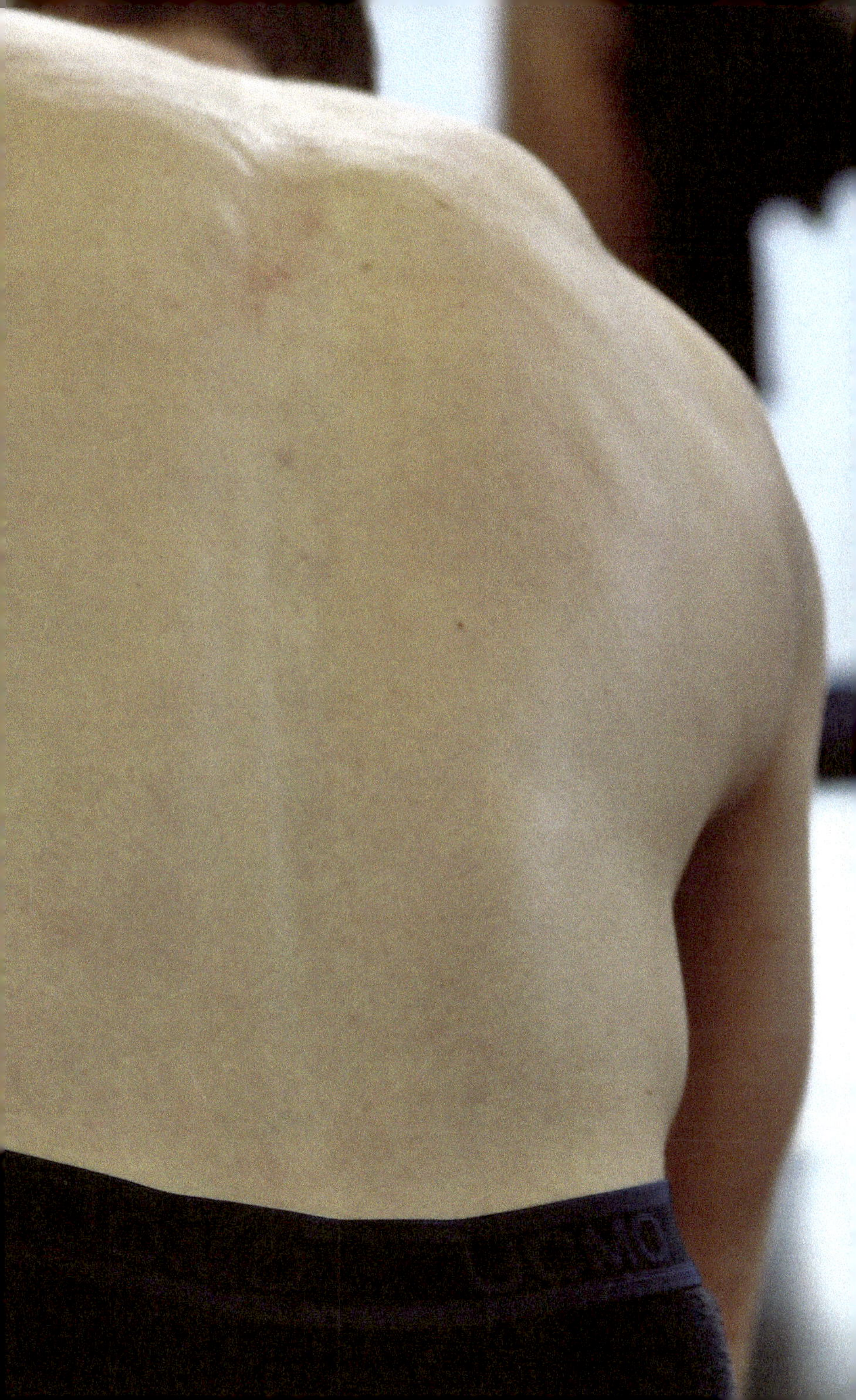

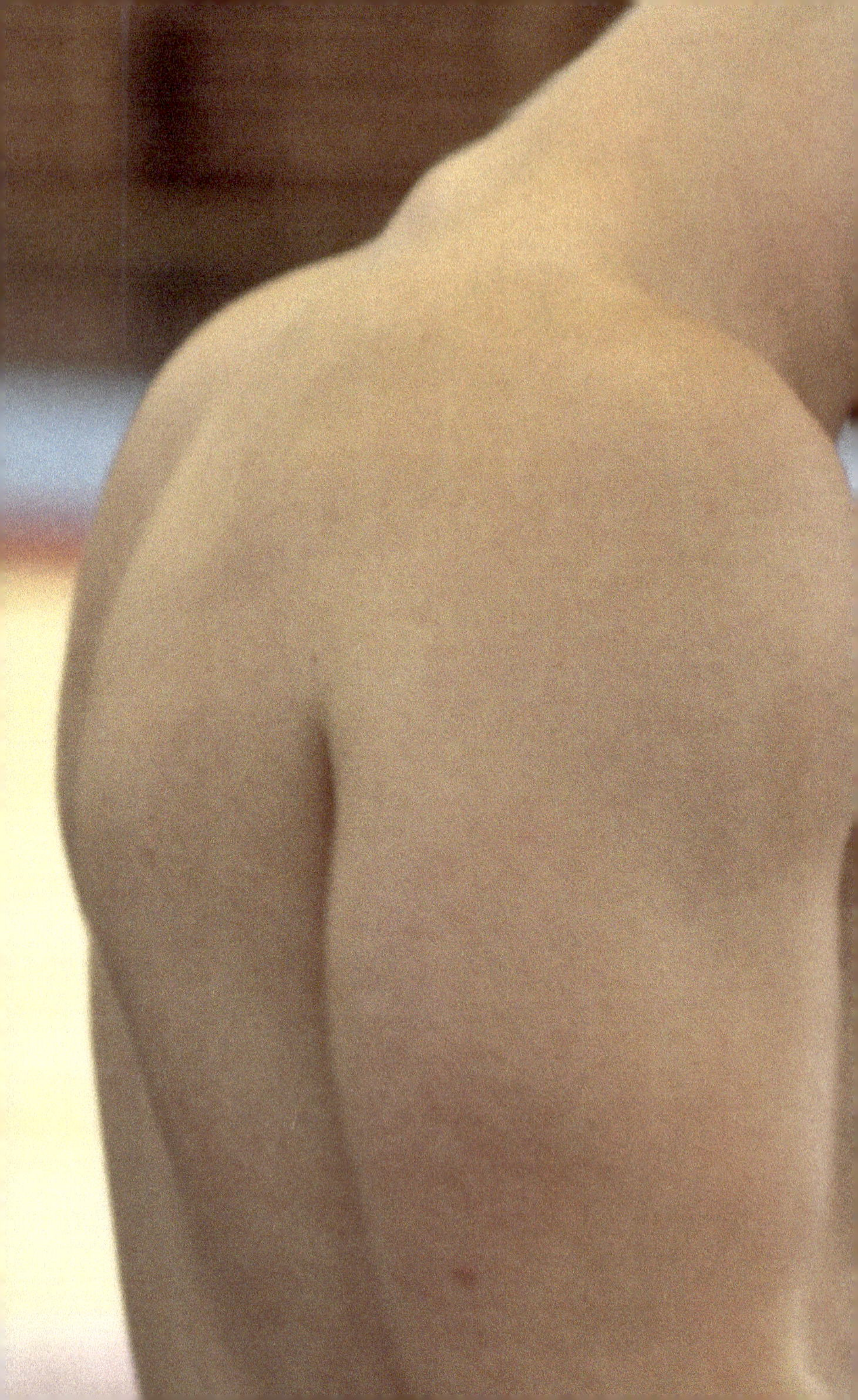

WEBER

spa

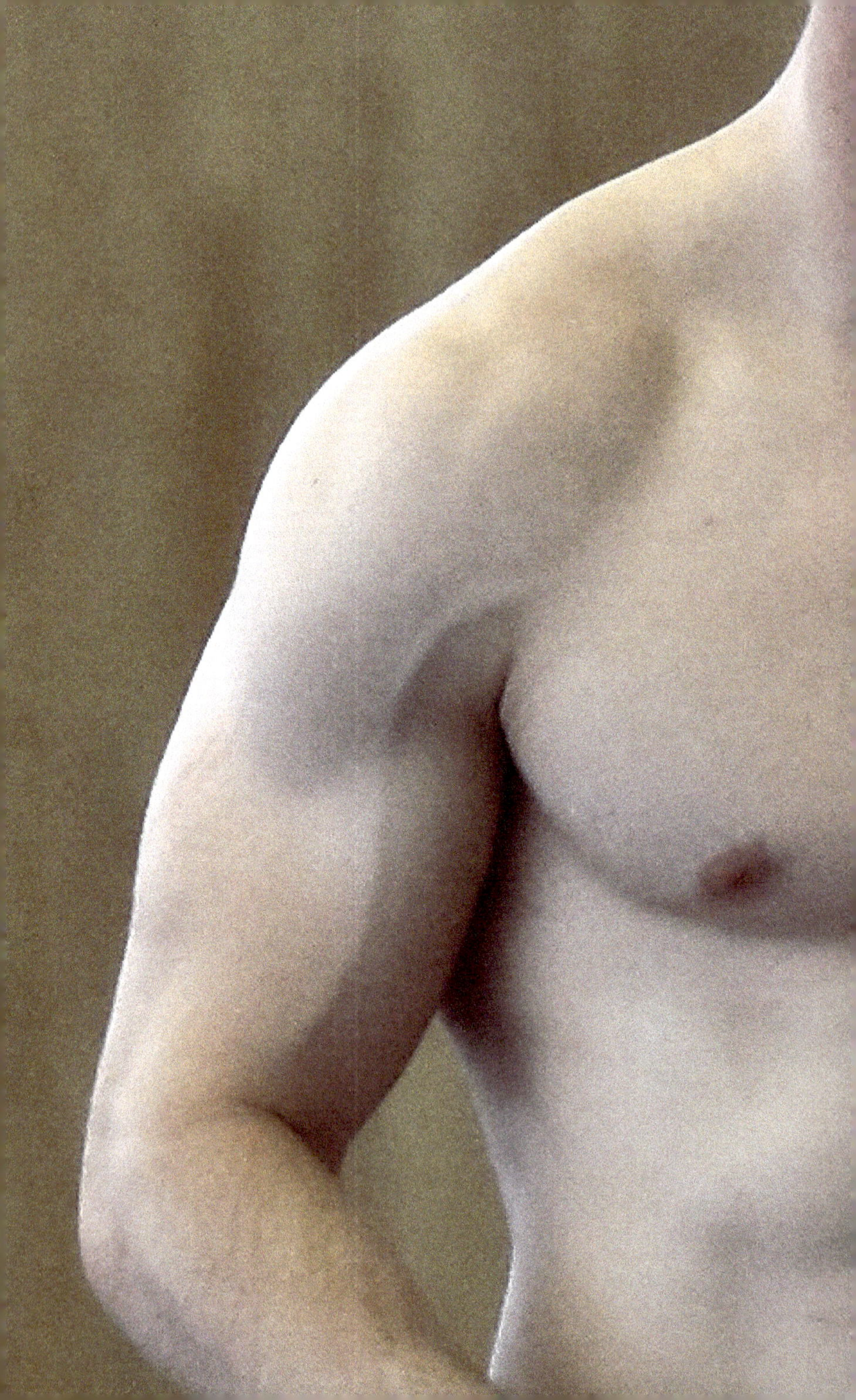

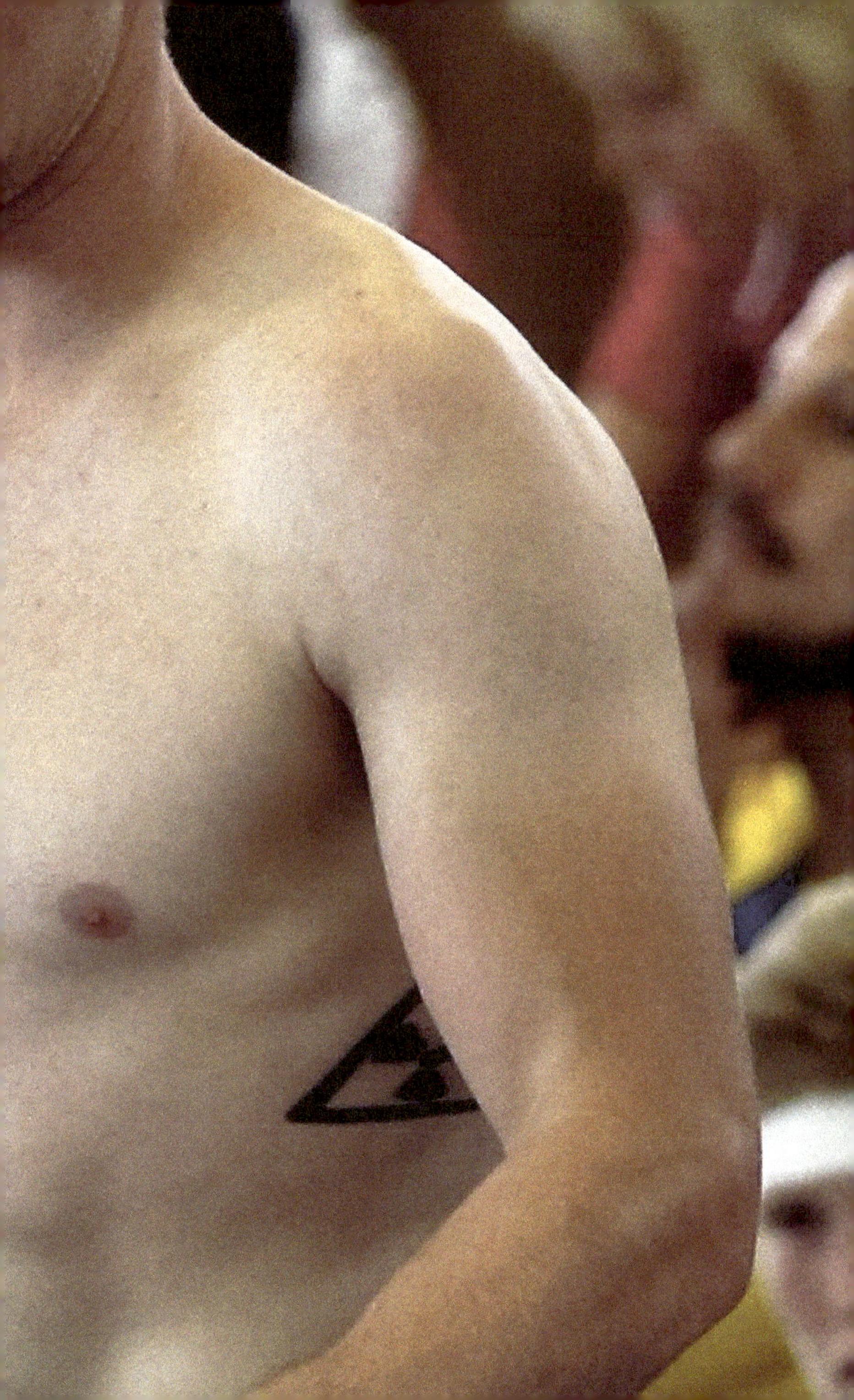

CPSIA information can be obtained
at www.ICGtesting.com
Printed in the USA
BVHW091304270619
552120BV00016B/531/P

9 780368 939860